Donated by
Editorial Directions
in honor of
The Koutris Family
to the
Olive-Mary Stitt LMC
2003-2004

Florence Nightingale

SPIRIT
of America®

FLORENCE *Nightingale*

FOUNDER OF THE NIGHTINGALE SCHOOL OF NURSING

By Marc Davis

Content Adviser: Manon Parry, Curator of Historical Exhibitions,
History of Medicine Division, National Library of Medicine,
Bethesda, Maryland

The Child's World®
Chanhassen, Minnesota

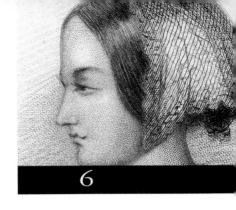

6

FLORENCE *Nightingale*

Published in the United States of America by The Child's World®
PO Box 326 • Chanhassen, MN 55317-0326 • 800-599-READ • www.childsworld.com

Acknowledgments

The Child's World®: Mary Berendes, Publishing Director

Editorial Directions, Inc.: E. Russell Primm, Editorial Director; Pam Rosenberg, Line Editor; Elizabeth K. Martin, Assistant Editor; Olivia Nellums, Editorial Assistant; Susan Hindman, Copy Editor; Susan Ashley, Halley Gatenby, Proofreaders; Jean Cotterell, Kevin Cunningham, Peter Garnham, Fact Checkers; Tim Griffin/IndexServ, Indexer; Dawn Friedman, Photo Researcher; Linda S. Koutris, Photo Selector

Photo

Cover: Hulton Archive/Getty Images; Courtesy of the Clendening History of Medicine Library, University of Kansas Medical Center: 17; Hulton-Deutsch Collection/Corbis: 6, 18, 22, 27, 28; Robert Holmes/Corbis: 10; Historical Picture Archive/Corbis: 16; Corbis: 19; Stapleton Collection/Corbis: 20; Bettmann/Corbis: 21, 24; The Granger Collection, New York: 7, 8, 11 top, 15; Hulton Archive/Getty Images: 2, 11 bottom, 13, 23, 25 top and bottom; North Wind Picture Archives: 9, 12, 14.

Library of Congress Cataloging-in-Publication Data

Davis, Marc.
  Florence Nightingale : founder of the Nightingale School of Nursing / by Marc Davis.
     p. cm.
"Spirit of America."
Includes index.
Summary: Provides a brief introduction to Florence Nightingale, her accomplishments, and her impact on history.
  ISBN 1-59296-003-0
1. Nightingale, Florence, 1820–1910—Juvenile literature. 2. Nurses—England—Biography—Juvenile literature.
[1. Nightingale, Florence, 1820–1910. 2. Nurses. 3. Women—Biography.] I. Title.
  RT37.N5D383 2003
  610.73'092—dc21   2003004161

Contents

Chapter ONE

A Call to Service

Florence Nightingale was named after the city of Florence, Italy.

FLORENCE NIGHTINGALE CHANGED THE WAY nurses care for the sick and injured. She also changed the way hospitals are run. Through her work, she helped make nursing the skilled profession we know today.

Florence Nightingale was born in Florence, Italy, on May 12, 1820. Her parents, William Edward Nightingale and Frances "Fanny" Smith, were visiting Italy at the time of Florence's birth. They decided to name their daughter after the city in which she was born.

The Nightingales were rich, and they raised Florence in comfort in homes in Derbyshire, Hampshire, and near London, England. Florence had an older sister named Parthenope. Their father taught them French, Greek, German, Italian, and Latin. He also instructed them in history, mathematics, and philosophy. Florence enjoyed her studies and was a good student.

Florence and her sister had pets and toys and ponies. They were well dressed. They had a nurse and servants. Florence was intelligent, but she was also a day-dreamer with a lively imagination. Even though she should have had a happy child-hood, she often seemed troubled.

Florence and her sister Parthenope were members of a wealthy English family.

When she was 16, she believed that God had spoken to her and called her to service. Florence said that she had heard a voice. The voice told her that she would be needed for special work. But at the time, she did not know what it would be. She did not tell her family about the voice she heard and kept that secret to herself. Not until years later, when Florence wrote about it, would people learn of this experience.

By the spring of 1839, Florence's mother hoped that her daughter would soon be married. But Florence had no interest in getting married. She had yet to answer the call of God, and that disturbed her. Mathematics had always interested her, so she decided to concentrate on studying math. Frances became upset with Florence, thinking that young men would not be interested in a woman who studied a serious subject. Although Florence was now involved in her studies, she was not happy.

Florence Nightingale was a daydreamer who believed that God had spoken to her.

She still enjoyed going to balls and being the center of attention. At the same time, she wanted to do important work. This **conflict** troubled her, but it would soon be resolved.

In the summer months, the Nightingales would go to their other estate in Derbyshire in northern England.

Florence Nightingale enjoyed going to parties and balls.

Many poor people lived in small cottages near the Nightingale **mansion**. When Florence was a teenager she became interested in these people and their difficult lives. She visited them often, bringing them food and medicine they could not afford. For the first time, Florence felt that she had done something worthwhile.

Interesting Fact

▶ Parthenope, Florence's older sister, was born in Naples, Italy. Her name is pronounced "par-then-OH-pee."

9

Soon afterward, Florence experienced other events that suggested what her **mission** in life should be. She nursed her sick grandmother back to health. She spent time with her childhood nurse who was dying. She also took care of an orphan child. These activities satisfied Florence's deep desire to help other people. This was the work she wanted to do for the rest of her life. She decided to become a nurse.

Florence Nightingale knew that while some people in Derbyshire lived in mansions like this one, many others were poor and had difficult lives.

FLORENCE NIGHTINGALE'S PARENTS and their two young daughters returned to England in 1821. They settled at Lea Hurst, William Edward Nightingale's family home in Derbyshire. Lea Hurst was near the Nightingale lead smelter, which operated throughout Florence's lifetime. The family lived in this home full-time until 1823 and continued to spend summers there throughout Florence's childhood.

Florence was a sickly child, possibly as a result of her exposure to lead from the smelter. One of the symptoms of lead poisoning is weakness of the wrists. Florence did not learn to write until she was 11 or 12 years old because of what she called "a weakness in my hands."

In 1823, the Nightingale family moved to Kynsham Court in Herefordshire. Two years later, the family moved to a mansion in Hampshire called Embley Park. This was the Nightingale family's main home. Embley Park remained a private residence until 1946, when Embley Park School was founded. Although the former Nightingale home is now a school, few changes have been made to the building and grounds. Once each year, near Florence's birthday on May 12, visitors can tour Embley Park.

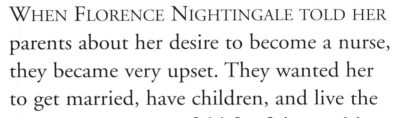

Chapter Two

Florence Nightingale Spreads Her Wings

Nursing was not considered a respectable job when Florence Nightingale was a young woman.

WHEN FLORENCE NIGHTINGALE TOLD HER parents about her desire to become a nurse, they became very upset. They wanted her to get married, have children, and live the peaceful life of the wealthy. Well-to-do English women in those days did not work, and they certainly did not work as nurses. Nursing was not thought of as respectable work because it involved **domestic** chores and was considered servants' work. Nightingale, however, would not change her mind. But to study nursing, she would have to go to a hospital.

Hospitals in the 1840s were often dirty, **unsanitary** places. The **wards** smelled unpleasant. Patients did not have bathrooms. Their bedsheets were not changed regularly. Medicine was not available for pain and other problems. Patients often died from medical problems that would be easily cured today. Rich people could afford to be treated in their homes. Hospitals were mainly for the poor.

In the 1840s, hospitals were often crowded, dirty places.

Several years would pass before Nightingale could begin her training. Meanwhile, she read reports and books about hospitals and health, and learned about these subjects. At the same time, she continued to attend the parties and balls her mother enjoyed so much.

Twice during this period, two young men wanted to marry Nightingale. She refused both of them. Marriage would only get in the way of her wish to become a nurse. Her parents and sister were very worried about her refusal to marry and about her desire to work as a nurse.

To get away from her family for a while, Nightingale spent a few months in late 1849 and 1850 taking a trip with friends. They traveled to Egypt and Europe. She visited some hospitals during the trip, where she watched how nurses took care of the sick and injured.

Not long after she returned to England, Nightingale met the person who would change everything for her: Dr. Elizabeth Blackwell, the first woman to become a licensed physician. Blackwell was visiting England. After their meeting, Nightingale was more determined than ever to become a nurse.

Florence Nightingale traveled to Egypt in 1849.

In 1851, Nightingale went to a hospital in Kaiserswerth, Germany, to begin her training. She had heard about this hospital and visited it during her trip the previous year. It was run by an organization called the Institution of Protestant Deaconesses. There, women took **vows** similar to the religious vows taken by nuns. Nuns had a long history of caring for the poor and the sick. Their work appealed to Nightingale because she saw nursing as a spiritual calling. At Kaiserswerth, she became a fully trained nurse. This was just the beginning of her achievements.

Nightingale took an unpaid job in 1853 running a hospital in London. Her father

Elizabeth Blackwell was the first woman to attend medical school and become a licensed physician. She was an inspiration to Florence Nightingale.

In 1853, Nightingale visited many hospitals in London and gave advice to nurses.

paid her an allowance while she did this. Her family was trying to understand what she wanted to do with her life. Taking charge of all the details necessary to run a hospital, Nightingale gained valuable experience, both as a nurse and as a manager. She made many changes in the way the hospital was run, both in the wards and in the way nurses handled the patients.

During this time, Nightingale also visited other hospitals in London. When a **cholera** epidemic swept through London, she advised nurses on how to care for patients who had become sick. She was very successful but wanted bigger **challenges**. She would soon face a terrible challenge unlike anything she had seen before.

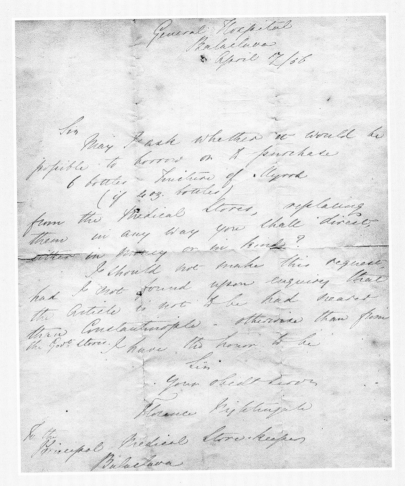

THROUGHOUT HER LONG life, Florence Nightingale wrote many letters. They were sent to government officials, army officers, doctors, nurses, family members, and friends.

Some of her letters are housed in a collection at the Clendening Library at the University of Kansas in Kansas City. The letters show her many different interests. Among her main concerns were army hospitals and health and medical matters. One of her long letters was a report to the British government's War Office on army hospitals. The War Office was in charge of the British army. As a result of her letter, changes were made in army hospitals that helped many sick and wounded soldiers recover more quickly.

In some of her letters, Nightingale asks for advice on medical care, nursing, and hospital management. In other letters, she gives advice on these matters. One of her letters also included a design for a 120-bed hospital.

Some letters give a more personal view of Nightingale. They contain her opinions on music, cooking, and the need for teaching geography and religion to young people.

Chapter THREE

The "Angel of Mercy"

IN MARCH 1854, LESS THAN A YEAR AFTER Florence Nightingale took the job in London, the British and French entered the Crimean War. This war was fought in an area called the Crimea on the Black Sea, across from Turkey. The Turks had declared war on Russia the previous year when the Russians sent their navy to the Crimea in an attempt to take land from Turkey. The British and French wanted to help the Turks stop the Russians.

Soon after the war started, Nightingale volunteered to go to the

The city of Balaklava on the Black Sea was a supply port for the British, French and Turkish armies during the Crimean War.

Crimea to care for wounded troops. The British secretary of war asked her if she would take a group of nurses with her. The government promised to pay for everything. Nightingale began looking for nurses. At first, she was unable to find enough women with the right training and experience. However, she wasn't sure what skills the nurses would need because no one was sure exactly what the nurses would face in the Crimea. Even-

These women are carrying luggage for the nurses traveling to Scutari to work with Florence Nightingale during the Crimean War.

tually, she hired 38 women and in November 1854 brought them to Turkey. Some of the women were from religious orders and some were from ordinary hospitals. She permitted the nuns to wear their **habits** and made the nurses wear a uniform of a white cap and a gray dress. The nurses were all paid the same salary and lived together in the same rooms.

Nightingale and the nurses stayed in a Turkish city called Scutari. The war was being fought nearby. Although she had known of the many problems at the Scutari Barrack Hospital, she was shocked by what she saw there.

Conditions were terrible. There were shortages of beds, medical supplies, and equipment. Soldiers lay side-by-side in overcrowded wards suffering from pain and disease and dying of their wounds. The entire hospital was dirty and smelled. Doctors and medicine were scarce. There were no nurses until Nightingale and her nurses arrived. Conditions on the battlefield were equally bad, with little food or equipment for the troops.

Although the British generals had tried to downplay these problems to keep up morale back home, a newspaper reporter named William Howard Russell wrote about

Florence Nightingale and her nurses worked at the Scutari Barrack Hospital.

them in *The Times* of London. Nightingale had read these articles before she went to the Crimea. When the news reported that Nightingale was taking nurses to the Crimea to care for wounded British soldiers, Russell was allowed to travel with them. His reports in *The Times* raised awareness of the situation and money to help her pay for supplies and nurses.

William Howard Russell was a newspaper reporter who wrote about the poor conditions soldiers faced in the Crimea. His reports helped raise money to pay for supplies and nurses.

The doctors that Nightingale had to work with at Scutari at first were not helpful or friendly. They didn't approve of a wealthy woman like her running a hospital for soldiers. They did not permit her or her nurses to go into the wards where they were most needed.

The nurses' quarters were very small and had rats and lice. The women had nothing to eat, no beds, and no light. But Nightingale was not discouraged. She immediately started trying to improve hospital conditions. She assigned different jobs to the nurses, cooked meals for the patients and doctors, and sent patients' dirty clothes out to be washed. Still, the doctors did not allow the nurses into the wards. Nevertheless, Nightingale was patient. She was sure that soon she and her group would be able to properly tend to the sick and wounded soldiers.

As winter set in, the terrible toll of starvation, injury, disease, and exhaustion became overwhelming. Even when troops had won individual battles, many soldiers had been killed and many more were injured. Many became sick in the cold. As the wounded were brought into the already crowded hospital, the doctors finally realized they needed the help of Nightingale and her nurses.

When Nightingale entered the hospital wards for the first time, she was shocked by what she saw. Never had she seen anything so horrible. But she went to work

Many soldiers were killed and wounded in the bloody battles of the Crimean War.

right away to improve conditions. She ordered food and clothing, medical supplies, soap, mattresses, and other necessary equipment. She used her own money and the influence of her powerful friends back home to get supplies quickly. The materials were shipped from the nearby city of Constantinople. Today, that city is called Istanbul and is the largest city in Turkey.

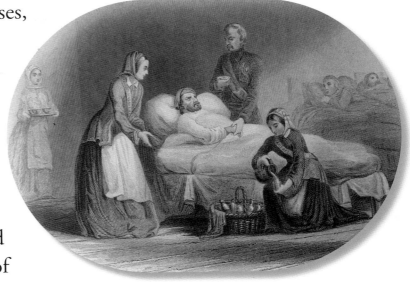

Florence Nightingale and her nurses worked hard to improve conditions at the hospital in Scutari.

At the same time the supplies were ordered, Nightingale, her nurses, and other workers began cleaning the filthy hospital. The bathrooms and plumbing were repaired. Dirty wards, including the floors, were washed. Soiled clothing, sheets, and blankets were laundered.

Just as important was the task of attending to the wounded. Nightingale and her nurses changed bandages, fed patients medicine and food, and made sure their beds were clean. Slowly but surely, the hospital was cleaned up.

Florence Nightingale became known as the "lady with a lamp."

Needed supplies became available. The men's suffering was relieved as much as possible under the circumstances.

But there was always more work to be done. Nightingale would sometimes be awake for 24 hours. When she was not in the wards, she was busy writing letters and reports, and attending to the other tasks involved in running a hospital.

At night, when no nurses were allowed into the wards, Nightingale went from patient to patient, spending a few minutes with each. She would take care of their wounds or offer a few words of comfort. She carried a lamp on her nightly rounds. The patients began calling her "the lady with a lamp." Later, she became known as an "angel of mercy."

As the months went by and hospital conditions got better, Nightingale won the respect and admiration of the wounded men, the doctors she worked with, and the nurses she supervised.

THE CRIMEAN WAR STARTED IN October 1853 and ended in February 1856. The British, French, and Turks fought the Russians. Most of the fighting took place on the Crimea, a peninsula, or piece of land, surrounded on three sides by the Black Sea. The land was part of Russia. Like many wars, the reasons for it were complicated.

The battles were bloody. Although the British, French, and Turks won the war, they lost many soldiers. Thousands of troops were killed and wounded on the battlefield. Many thousands more died in the hospitals of their wounds. But disease was the biggest killer. About 250,000 men on each side died during the war, and the majority of these died as a result of illness. Without the help of Florence Nightingale and her nurses, many more would have died.

Years of Hard Work and Honor

FLORENCE NIGHTINGALE HAD BECOME A national heroine to the British public, which had read about her work in the Crimea. In running the army hospital, Nightingale had managed a large and vital medical organization in very difficult circumstances. She had done so despite shortages of supplies and money. Her work had shown that women should not be excluded from important careers.

But the strain of working so hard for so long soon made Nightingale sick. In the spring of 1855, she almost died. As she lay ill, her fame grew even more. Queen Victoria of England sent Nightingale a gift. Her family, which did not fully approve of her career before the war, was very proud now because of the national attention she was receiving.

Part of Florence Nightingale's success in revolutionizing nursing came from her wealthy background. She made nursing a respectable career by being a respectable woman even before she established training to raise standards in nursing. Nightingale, however, paid little attention to the public praise and honors that came her way. She was interested only in her work.

Nurses lunch at Nightingale House at St. Thomas' Hospital in London

Nightingale recovered from her sickness and worked for the reform of all army hospitals. She started a letter-writing campaign and gave advice to the government committees that were formed to consider making the necessary changes. Now her main interest became the health and well-being of British soldiers. After studying conditions in the British army, including hospitals, she wrote an important book on that subject. Many of the recommendations in her book were used to improve the health, diet, and barracks of British soldiers.

She also established the Nightingale Training School for Nurses at St. Thomas'

Interesting Fact

▸ Nurses who trained at the Nightingale nursing school at St. Thomas' Hospital in London studied for a year. Then they worked on the hospital wards for two more years and wrote reports on their daily activities.

> Florence Nightingale is buried at the church of St. Margaret in East Wellow, Hampshire, England.

Florence Nightingale helped make nursing the respectable profession it is today.

Hospital in London. The nurses trained at this school were known as Nightingale Nurses. They were sent around the world to teach the new methods of nursing. Her famous name put these nurses in high demand. From this time on, nursing gradually grew over the years to become a respected and admired profession. Specialized training became necessary as the nursing profession became more technical and medical in nature.

Again, Nightingale became sick. This time she did not completely recover. For the rest of her life, she lived in a weakened condition. Doctors could not say exactly what was wrong with her. Nevertheless, she continued her work. She spent her days lying on a couch, working, writing letters, and talking with visitors.

As the years went by, Nightingale continued working but gradually became blind. In 1907, King Edward VII of England awarded her the Order of Merit. She was the first woman to ever receive this high honor. On August 13, 1910, Florence Nightingale died at the age of 90. She is remembered as a pioneer in public health. The books and letters she wrote are still read by nurses and other health professionals.

1820　Florence Nightingale is born on May 12, 1820, in Florence, Italy.

1837　Nightingale believes she hears a call from God on February 7. The voice tells her she has a special mission in life.

1849　Nightingale takes a trip with friends to Egypt and Europe.

1851　Nightingale studies nursing at the hospital in Kaiserswerth, Germany.

1853　The Crimean War begins. Nightingale takes an unpaid job running a London hospital.

1854　The British and French enter the Crimean War in March. Nightingale arrives at the British army hospital in Turkey on November 3.

1855　Nightingale becomes sick and nearly dies.

1856　The Crimean War ends, and Nightingale returns home as a national heroine.

1859　*Notes on Hospitals* is published.

1860　*Notes on Nursing* is published, and the Nightingale Training School for Nurses opens.

1870　Nightingale helps start the National Society for Aid to the Sick and Wounded, the precursor to the British Red Cross.

1907　The British Order of Merit is awarded to Nightingale, the first woman in history to ever receive this high honor from the British monarchy.

1910　Nightingale dies on August 13.

challenges (CHAL-uhnj-es)
Challenges are things that require a lot of work or extra effort to do. Florence Nightingale enjoyed meeting the challenges of her work.

cholera (KOL-ur-uh)
A serious disease that causes severe diarrhea. Florence Nightingale told other nurses how to care for people with cholera.

conflict (KON-flict)
A conflict is a disagreement. The conflict between Florence Nightingale's wealthy lifestyle and her desire to do important work troubled her.

domestic (duh-MESS-tik)
Something that is domestic has to do with the home. Nursing was not considered a respectable career because it involved doing domestic chores.

habits (HAB-its)
Habits are long, loose dresses worn by nuns. The nuns who went to the Crimea with Florence Nightingale were allowed to wear their habits.

mansion (MAN-shuhn)
A mansion is a very large house. The Nightingales lived in a mansion.

mission (MISH-uhn)
A mission is a special job given to someone. Florence Nightingale believed that she had been given a special mission in life.

unsanitary (uhn-SAN-uh-ter-ee)
Something that is unsanitary is not clean and filled with germs. Hospitals in the early 1800s were often unsanitary.

vows (VOUS)
Vows are very serious promises or commitments. The nurses at Kaiserswerth made vows similar to those made by nuns.

wards (WORDS)
Wards are large rooms in hospitals where many patients are cared for. Florence Nightingale was shocked by the conditions she saw in some hospital wards.

For Further INFORMATION

Web Sites

Visit our homepage for lots of links about Florence Nightingale:
http://www.childsworld.com/links.html

Note to Parents, Teachers, and Librarians:
We routinely verify our Web links to make sure they're safe,
active sites—so encourage your readers to check them out!

Books

Barnham, Kay. *Florence Nightingale: The Lady of the Lamp.* Austin, Tex.:
Raintree/Steck Vaughn, 2002.

Gorrell, Gena K. *Heart and Soul: The Story of Florence Nightingale.* Toronto:
Tundra Books, 2000.

Malam, John. *Florence Nightingale.* Chicago: Heinemann Library, 2001.

Places to Visit or Contact

The Florence Nightingale Museum
To learn more about the life and work of Florence Nightingale
2 Lambeth Palace Road
London, SE1 7EW
(44) 171-620-0374

U.S. National Library of Medicine
*To write for more information about Florence Nightingale and other famous
pioneers in the field of medicine*
History of Medicine Division
8600 Rockville Pike
Bethesda, MD 20894
301/594-5983

Index

About the Author

MARC DAVIS IS A FORMER NEWSPAPER REPORTER, THE AUTHOR of two novels, and a freelance journalist specializing in business, medical, historical, and cultural subjects. His writing-reporting has appeared in national publications and on the Internet. He attended the University of Illinois, Chicago, and New York University. Davis lives in a Chicago suburb.